Also by Gus Speth

Red Sky at Morning: America and the Crisis of the Global Environment

The Bridge at the Edge of the World: Capitalism, the Environment, and Crossing from Crisis to Sustainability

America the Possible: Manifesto for a New Economy

Angels by the River: A Memoir

What We Have Instead

poems by Gus Speth

What We Have Instead

poems by Gus Speth

SHIRES PRESS

What We Have Instead
Poems
©2019 Gus Speth

ISBN: 978-1-60571-457-8

Editorial advisor, Emma Irving
Design/production, Anne Pace
Cover art by the author

Printed in the United States
May, 2019

This book is available from
Amazon.com, barnesandnoble.com, Ingram,
and indie bookstores across the country at **IndieBound.org**

For Cece

Contents

1 Dreaming Up a Future

New Farm 3
What We Have Instead 4
What He Could Have Done 5
Banners Yet To Be Unfurled (Song).......................6
A Place of Little Pretense 8
In Bed 10
Thought Police 11
Thinking Like a Mountain 12
Vision on the Beach 14
The Id Is 15
I Know You Want To Cry 16
Soul Searching 18

2 Love Story

I Voices 21
II With a Name Like That 22
III Billy Ballou 23
IV The Mistake: Merv's Story 26
V A Letter from the Nation's Capital 28
VI You Remind Me 29
VII Old Sam's Story 30
VIII Speaking of Home 32
IX A Morning Around New Year's Day 34
X Somewhere Lovely 36

3 Celebrations

American Acropolis *41*
Sarah's Farewell *42*
Spring Suspended *43*
Celebration *44*
Happy Ending. Not! *46*
Springtime *47*
Friendship *48*
Delmarva *50*
All the Color *52*
A Dog's Life *54*
Fast Breeder *55*

4 The Proper Order of the World

Holding It All Together *59*
New Morning *60*
airborne *61*
Not Far From the Tree *62*
The Evening News *65*
Smoky *66*
Forgiveness *67*
Crepuscular Thoughts *68*
Fishing with the Family *69*
A Balanced Life *70*
The Promise *71*

All persons named in the poems in this volume are fictional except Aldo Leopold, Pete Seeger, Ned Coffin, Cameron and Gus Speth, Amelia and Gus Speth Sr., the TV personalities mentioned in the poem The Evening News, Albert Camus, Dylan Thomas, Martin Luther King, and the Sewee.

Preface

I started writing poems a few years ago. Though I had no real plans, I have enjoyed writing and sharing them. When I strike a chord with someone, I think, wow, this is a very nice way to reach through to another person.

After a life of writing legal briefs, books, and other documents for environmental causes, I thought it was time—maybe too late!—to give my right brain a chance. In these poems I have tried to write about the world around me, and around us, using our remarkable language as strongly and concisely as I can.

Some poems I read leave me wondering what they are about. You will not have that challenge here. I hope I get some smiles from you, nods of recognition, and maybe a tear or two.

So many people have helped me with this effort. I am grateful every day for them.

There is a story in section 2 of these poems. It is mostly about people who, with quiet strength, persevered. If you read this part from start to finish, you will see the story. But I will be complimented if you choose to read any of these poems at all.

Gus Speth
Strafford, Vermont
Spring 2019

1

Dreaming Up a Future

New Farm

So, this is
what we have:
a young couple
who can feel
the green grass
in their toes
know the proper
order of things
of hills to home
and barn shaped
to fields and woods
and the beauty
of enough space
to see the full scene
so that they now can
envision a time
when sheep played
white and brown
dots into the distance
of a past
not very far away.
Not far at all.

What We Have Instead

In this our world

if there is meaning
we create it.

If there is community
we build it.

If there is justice
we forge it.

If there is providence
we provide it.

If there is love
we extend it.

Nothing is given
save life itself.

We have only
this speck of earth
and each other.

It is enough.

So let us pray
to fields and friends
and to the spacious sky.

What He Could Have Done

He could have pitched a tent in Lafayette Square
and fasted until action was taken on climate change.
He thought about it many times, imagined reporters
seeking his views as he sat outside his little tent.

Yet even his fantasy moved to the
possibility of fasting away instead in a
Hay-Adams room overlooking the park.
No reason not to be comfortable, and besides
he would get more reporters that way.
Along with water, he thought:
should I take a vitamin pill every day?

Amid the great suffering of the world,
he had lived a life of worldly comfort.
He did a bit of time in jail for protesting
the end of the world as we know it.

Not risking everything is a strategy
that ends with grandkids deprived.
He knows that now, deeply knows
this is no time for self-deception.
But will he act on his conviction?

Banners Yet To Be Unfurled (Song)

The snow lies lightly on the lilacs
round by the kitchen door.
The juncos peck in stone cracks
endless in their search for more.

I think that is my way too,
to keep the search going on.
What else really could I do
but find new ways to scorn?

As Camus said of Sisyphus
who toiled with his stone,
there is no fate for us
that can't be beat by scorn.

And so I scorn what passes here today
for equality and justice before the law,
for helping the poor to find a way,
for promises the troops will soon withdraw.

The politicians are pathetic souls;
almost every sentence is a lie.
Recognition is their main goal.
To integrity they've said good-bye.

Oh purple mountain majesty!
Oh fruited plains of amber grain!
The machine crushes endlessly
everything for investment's gain.

And so we search for ways to fight.
We see the beauty of the snow,
but we know to make it right
may require our blood to flow.

We've seen the heads bandaged round,
the men and women teared by gas.
Each has earned a special crown.
They know the system will not last.

Scorn, rage, and many actions:
protests coming round the world.
Today we see but a fraction
of banners yet to be unfurled!

A Place of Little Pretense

This small beach house was built in 1951,
just across the dunes from the big breakers.
Facing the full Atlantic through a few palmettos,
it has survived the ferocity of many encounters,
including the direct hit of the big storm Hugo.
It has survived thousands of children
tracking in tons of sand in wet bathing suits.
It has been the enduring strong cauldron
for explosions of laughter and love and anger.
Its tiny kitchen has seen the endless shucking
of local oysters and the frying of many flounder.

How many books have been read here?
How much coffee spilled into the rugs?
How many exhibitions of grandkids' art?
How many hugs?
How many castles washed away by the waves?
How many games of Monopoly and cards?
How many kids bodysurfed to dad's legs?
How many carbs?
How many shark teeth found near the surf?
How many dogs slept in the chairs?
How many bare feet warmed by the sand?
How many beers?

The signs of age are all around:
tiny worn sinks in upstairs bedrooms,
a bottom floor flat on the ground,
a very small toilet in the bathroom,
the walls and ceiling a simple bare pine,
the medicine cabinet with its slit in the back,
the razor blades there to oblivion assigned.
There is mold around the edges and corners,
lots of rust from sitting in the salty air,
and boards worn out around the dormers.

This house is a modest place on the beach,
yet pilgrims trek here each summer.
It's a state of mind they hope to reach,
to see again their families and each other,
to watch birds and catch some fish,
to worship the tanning sun,
and the boys look at girls, and wish.

In Bed

My dog has positional anxiety.
He awakes and moves quite quietly
around and around and around
making small circles on his bed,
searching for just the right place
to put first his rear then his head,
one that feels satisfactory.

Complicating the situation
is his friend on the cushion.
Once a pup barely tolerated,
she's now too big a friend
to be pushed and relegated
to a small corner at the end.

If a dog can worry so
about taking the right position
and how to relate to another,
imagine then the human condition
when it comes to sharing the cover.

Thought Police

Are the thought police around?
Yes, well please bring them in.
Have a seat, anywhere. Some tea?
Once I thought my thoughts were good,
but now they cry out for policing.
My anger needs modulating.
My hopes need lifting.
My vision of societal decline
definitely needs a bottoming.
Do you have experience
with others in this situation?
Have you prescribed TV?
Perhaps House of Cards?
Or The Handmaid's Tale?
Or The Night Of?
The Wire and Breaking Bad
were more upbeat. Maybe them?
Buying things, you say. Shopping.
You know I've thought of that!
Do you provide money?
Okay. I understand. Let's move on.
You say hard work then. Hmm.
You mean like in the yard?
Or for pay, like a barista?
I've got my doubts about that.
I already work two barista jobs.
Can we settle on a puppy?

Thinking Like a Mountain

Aldo Leopold knew nature
like few before or after.
He urged those who listened
"to think like a mountain."

Well, hell, I say, I am a mountain!
I am Storm King, here beside the Hudson,
a sentinel with which to reckon.

From my shining east flank I
often heard Pete Seeger singing,
notes forming tunes and rising
from the bow of the sloop Clearwater
as it tacked the Highland's wind gate.
From far on my top I've seen
many times, way past when,
Clearwater and Pete were strongest
sailing upstream against the wind.

Pete sang to all the parts of me,
not just my verdant slopes rising steep
from the fast-flowing river, but the parts that
move around, rub brown fur against
the parts that sink deep in me and share
my waters and my nourishment.
I give it freely, as do critters too small to see.
They too are part of me.

My leaves shimmer in chartreuse,
for spring I am bringing back.
I want to hear the ovenbird again,
to help the goldfinch find its gold,
to see soon the evening grosbeak
dancing among my limbs and leaves.

If you want to think like a mountain,
you must come to see me whole.
Energy flows coursing through me;
life each day from entropy stole.

Can you come to see me sacred,
all the beauty consecrated?
I am alive and fertile and fecund,
providing sustenance and refuge.

I know then what I am,
what I do in this world,
how to weather many threats,
how yet to sing back to the river,
how I am old, yes also that.
But even now I, Storm King,
am not clear on all that we
mountains are supposed to think.
I have told what Aldo meant.
Perhaps that is enough.
But there may be other thoughts,
thoughts waiting to be remembered.

Vision on the Beach

We were walking on the chilly beach this morning.
The sea calm, the small waves moseyed onto the shore.
Then, with a strange confluence of small breakers,
the surf shot skyward, and in the spreading spray
I saw the shape of Jesus walking on the water.
I let that sink in, and then I told my wife.
"What did He say?" she asked, seeming serious.
"Nothing," I replied. "He was walking away."

The Id Is

The Id is
and dwells among us.
It moves across the void
of moral reckoning.

It blocks light
and light vanishes.
It shreds truth
and truth vanishes.
It crushes hope
and hope vanishes.

Evil spreads around us
as hate and violence
and ignorance.
It has no delight,
no joy, no beauty.

Can there be a reckoning?
A confrontation with evil?
A community says yes,
and then others, many more,
for there are still
domains of truth
shards of light
people of great hope
weary but alive in the world.

I Know You Want To Cry

There is failure around me,
a glass of cheap wine
spilled onto the crisp resume.
"Accomplishments" blurring into the paper,
fading, disappearing.

Fifty years now of hard-striving
and the class moron is
erasing the blackboard.

Our common home
and fellow Americans
are under assault. Yet
the loss is applauded
by many of our people,
people with whom I would
gladly share a drink,
go to the movies, laugh.
People I know because
I have lived with them.
And, even worse, I did not
see it coming. Not like this.

What is to be done?
Cry? Done that.
Tune it out? Tried that.
Smash the TV with a big vase?
Maybe next.
But, really, really,
the only meaningful answer
is to pull oneself out of grief,
regret, anger, resignation, whatever,
and in every way we know
fight to take back our country
while her lingering light still shines.

Soul Searching

Our souls are somewhere,
waiting for us to find them.
Perhaps there is a way.

Such searched-for souls
embody the best of
who we are, and can be.

We speak of lost souls:
what a tragedy to have
lost our better selves.

We say she has a big soul.
She is whole then, complete.
She has found the way.

Her way is a path
that leads along the river
under the tall cypress
to a spot where you can hold hands
and wade into the current,
watching the dark waters flow.
Then it heads uphill to
the big pavilion on the bluff
where the door opens
to a place of memory
and old friends await and smile
on the other side.

2

Love Story

CAST

Amelia and Gus Speth Sr.
Cameron and Gus Speth
Summer Reyes
Billy Ballou and his mother Mabel
Merv, his sister Sis, and his niece Sally
Ethel, a friend of Mabel's
Sam and his wife Molly
Jonathan Countryman and his wife Jennifer

I   *Voices*

While the peepers perfume the twilight air
and the barred owl sings her simple song,
we rock gently, slowly on the old porch and
in the gathering darkness listen for voices.

Who, who speaks for you? Who speaks for you?

For the longest forever it was mother.
I hear her now at dawn, helping with
homework I was too tired for last night.
Where would I be if she were not there,
and now here on this sofa beside me?

Who, who speaks for you? Who speaks for you?

Dad is a ragamuffin, a mop of happy gray hair,
a jokester who keeps running the soft
soothing patter of simple laughter.
He tells the Principal he will keep me straight
and military school will not be needed.

Who, who speaks for you? Who speaks for you?

Time evaporates into the peepers and slow rocking.
I am back at the beginning, and I hear another voice.
Don't worry, Miss Amelia, you got a fine boy.
He'll be something one day, I know it.

Who, who speaks for you? Who speaks for you?

There have been so many who spoke for me,
voices heard now over the dark transom of evening.
All along the long river of my life, there have
been angels who spoke kind words on my behalf.

Who, who speaks for you? Who speaks for you?

II *With a Name Like That*

Many long years ago
my wife Cameron and I
went to a spot in New Orleans
in the Marigny district
along Frenchmen Street.
Summer Reyes was there
singing beautifully with her band,
and I said to myself,
"Cameron is as good as Summer
and if I were her manager
and she had a name like Summer Reyes,
wow, we could really go places,
touring around and having fun."

Named Gus as I am, I'm
sensitive to these matters.
A friend in the UN once said
"You become your name."
Movies love Gus—for animals.
Soon I will be a mule or mouse.
It has occurred to me
that if I were instead named
Jonathan Countryman,
I might have made a
good life in politics.

III *Billy Ballou*

On a gorgeous spring day in '58
during the term of Ike Eisenhower,
Billy Ballou was born in east Mobile.
It was never clear why it happened.

Billy was raised by his mother Mabel
in a small rundown house near the shipyards.
She loved him without measure or reserve.
To him she was his angel from heaven.

She would gather him up in her big arms,
press him to her warm body and twirl round
and round and the house would shake on its blocks.
He held the joy of those moments with him.

With his curly black hair and soulful eyes
and his smile to light up the rainy sky,
he won the hearts of her small group of friends.
He tried to follow their tease and chatter.

Billy needed all the love he could get.
He was born deaf and said to be simple.
Deaf and dumb. He was called deaf and dumb.
He would see those words form and be angry.

His mother found a church school for the deaf
where the main goal was to teach them to speak.
Imagine speaking words you've never heard.
He tried but knew he was no good at it.

Billy was a happy kid all the same.
He found a dinghy washed up on the shore.
He taught himself to sail and would go out
for hours on the bay and the great Tensaw.

And he loved sitting in the small kitchen
while his mother was busy with cooking.
His mother told her friends that what Billy
lacked in hearing he made up in smelling.

When his mother would stir the red onions
with fresh ginger and garlic she could see
his face glow and that big bright smile come out.
"Boy's got a stubborn streak, too," May said once.

Soon after Billy turned 14 he found
his mother dead in her bed one morning.
May had died overnight of a bad heart.
Billy fell across her bed and he wept.

No real relatives could be found for Billy.
He was soon put into a foster home
that was far away from his neighborhood,
far away from all that he knew and loved.

Then, a few months later, hardly noticed,
young Billy simply disappeared from sight.

The authorities felt obligated
to search land and water for our Billy.
They did a reasonable job of it.
A home neighbor said he stayed in mostly.

They said: "if you hear a sweet but odd laugh,
you will have found him." "He could hardly talk."
"Something was wrong. Don't know how he got by."
"I sure do hope you find him soon. Nice kid."

A dinghy was found washed up down the bay
in the stretch between Daphne and Fairhope.
Some of Billy's things were tied tight in it;
it was clearly identified as his.

The story took hold that Billy Ballou
had sailed way out into the bay and drowned.
Some said it was probably for the best,
with his simplicity and no mother.

His mother's friends thought rather different.
He was a swimmer and smart as a whip.
They dreamed the boy would show up before long.
One of them would sing quietly to herself:

Oh Billy Ballou Billy Ballou
Where are you Billy Ballou
We miss you so where did you go
We pray for you Billy Ballou

*The Sewee Indians of coastal South Carolina,
having had enough of merchant middlemen,
loaded their canoes with their wares
and set out paddling to markets in England.
No one knows what became of them, but
they were searchers for something better.*

IV *The Mistake: Merv's Story*

There was an accident on the highway
early on Sunday morning, just yesterday,
not an interstate but a poor state road.
We had talked about it being a bad stretch.

I can hardly bring myself to tell this.
She was pregnant and so they're both gone now.
My house creaks and bangs from the cold and wind.
It was frozen hard like this yesterday.

My Sis was driving fast and hit black ice
on the curve near the Ace Hardware and slid
flat sideways into an oncoming truck.
He was carrying a load of white pine.

On Saturday night late she had over
a new guy she met in the bar in town,
a mistake way past a few too many.
He went about it in a rough mean way.

"I want the cute young one too," he said.
"That's my daughter," Sis yelled. "Forget it, jerk!"
But he forced Sally into the bathroom,
locked the door tight, and took his pleasure.

Come morning, Sis knew what she had to do.
With her dead husband's pistol beside her
on the old pickup seat, she headed out
to the place he was staying for the night.

When she hit the ice she was likely thinking
about where she should put the first bullet.
Perhaps she was thinking between his legs.
That is what I likely would be thinking.

Sally said my Sis held her tight all night,
told how she fought and got hit many times.
She cried, "I'm so sorry. I'm so sorry."
Her mom finally found the gun and left.

I have my gun but I have told the police.
For now, I'll give the cops a chance to act.
I'll take care of Sally as best I can.
But I have so little to offer her.

Sis should have gone to school but went to drugs.
She straightened out became a good mother.
She loved, protected and worked hard at it.
But she had a weak spot for drink and men.

I will miss her to the end of my days.
But Sally, my God, how can I help her?
How can we get beyond this awfulness
and claim a small place of peace in this world?

V *A Letter from the Nation's Capital*

Ethel was excited to receive Billy's letter;
that's been many a year.
And now she has another, with a clipping.
A heartbeat she can hear.

She was closest of all his mother's friends
and remembers Billy well.
The clip's photo shows Billy with a group
of protesters raising hell.

He was passing out food to them,
several smiling in return.
They gathered there to teach a lesson,
one way past time to learn.

The news clip is dated March 9 '88:
Students Demand Deaf President Now!
Gallaudet students are revolting;
they make a solemn vow.

They have shut the campus down
and made their four demands.
They see change coming for the deaf,
signing it with their hands.

With the clip is a note from Billy:
I am part of all this
and proud to be a student here at Gallaudet.
I seal this with a kiss.

VI *You Remind Me*

After fifty plus years of marriage,
you are reminding me…of me.
It is not a case of old people
getting more alike, like babies.
It's that we are now each
half of the same person
so that together we know
who owns the big orchard
and how to cook together
in this very small kitchen.
But as very nice as that is,
it's not all I am getting at.
It's also that now you can fly like me,
and I can fly like you, and there
are very special moments
when we are flying together
in a wonderful new way.

VII *Old Sam's Story*

Did you know Molly?
It was new summer's day,
bright and fresh that morning,
and she was in the garden
with her favorite flowers budding.
How she loved her roses,
almost as much as I loved her.
Now this longest day returns,
and she is gone.
The sunset brings shadows
to untended blooms.
Bluebirds pause and float
from post to ground.

Everybody knew Molly!
And they loved her too.
She was a woman in full,
if I may say that.
She would look you in the eye
and you were in that moment
everything to her.
Her daddy once said of her,
"Lord, Molly, you can charm
the lard out of a biscuit."
She charmed me every day.
And on this endless day,
she is gone.

Itching is between
the hurt and its healing,
and I am itching all over.
The loss of her surrounds me.
I am covered by memories
of her silver hair on my shoulder.
On this day she would have loved,
she is gone.

VIII *Speaking of Home*

My wife shouts to upstairs,
"I am putting on coffee."
I roll in the bed and reply,
"I am putting on airs!"
And think to myself
when was the last time
I heard a person say that?
You don't hear it here
because hardly anyone
puts on airs in Vermont.
Better to put on warm clothes.

Highfalutin is not the local way,
I think, drinking the coffee.
Politicians are plain-spoken.
The clothes aren't fancy,
nor are the cars and homes.
Well, anyhow, that's it mostly.
Folks are caring with the land,
the farms and forests, and the bogs,
and artists and craftsmen are
everywhere making beautiful things.
Proud people, but not prideful.

Now don't go having a hissy fit
because I'm idealizing Vermonters.
I got to get along with these people.
It isn't that hard since they are
not really the remote and taciturn
folks they are made out to be.
Some on a good day could even
talk the breath right out of you.

We have moved four times,
headed north from the South,
dragging along word baggage
and accents that don't fit.
Not since we left in 1964
have we found a place
that feels so much like home.

IX *A Morning Around New Year's Day*

Real Vermonters love
a morning like this,
a land of ice and snow,
clear, crisp, and 5 below.
The purple shadows
from big bare maples
reach out across
the slopes and rolls.
The big balsam bows
with her new white coat
while the birdhouses
wear their snowcaps
and the swings try out
their new white loads as
the wind gives easy pushes.
Once-green everything
now everywhere white
except the red of sumac.
The deer will browse at dusk
but now what moves are
chickadees flitting and flying
with their friends the juncos.
There are a few goldfinch
at the feeders, but they left
their gold somewhere safe.
The dogs bark when the
long-hanging roof ice
drops in a noisy plump.

It is a beautiful day
for a walk on the road
or to head out with
skis or snowshoes,
and also very nice to return
to a warm sweet-smelling house.

Still, my wife and I were raised in warmer climes.
In a month or so we will be chilled enough to
take out of the refrigerator and be enjoyed
by friends and family on the beach in Carolina.

X *Somewhere Lovely*

Jonathan Countryman sat on his porch
in Litchfield Beach in the late afternoon.
He had just finished his fifth and his last
term as state senator and was thinking.
Half into his Bloody Mary, he knew
he had accomplished some important things,
but not as much as he hoped at the start.
He became leader of the progressives,
but this was South Carolina after all.
That damn flag yet flies around the state.
But I am still vertical, he thought, still
vertical after all.

On that warm March day, Jennifer joined him.
Married for fifty-one years come July,
she knew what he was thinking, and she said,
"It was worth it. We made a difference.
Even if we didn't, it was still worth it.
All the effort, the trying…beautiful!
We should go out and celebrate. Tonight.
Somewhere lovely."

Jonathan had heard about a new place,
a casual restaurant that seemed perfect.
It was near Murrells Inlet up the beach,
so they made reservations and took off.
When they got there, the first thing they noticed
were the grounds—the beautiful landscaping.
The camellias were blooming pink and red.
An old man was bent over the roses,
clipping them expertly to get the best.
Jennifer was a gardener herself,
and he started talking roses with her.

"My apartment is down the road from here.
I volunteered to care for this garden.
My name is Sam. My wife loved her roses
and when I work here, I remember all
the good things with her. It is a blessing."

The restaurant was indeed quite lovely.
She's an attractive woman, Jonathan thought,
as they were warmly greeted at the door.
"Hello," she said, "and welcome to our place.
I'm Sally. I know about your service,
and I have admired it from afar.
This restaurant is something my husband
and I have long wanted, and here we are!
That's him over there where they are cooking
the best food on the coast, or so we claim!"

Jonathan could see an animated man
with curly gray hair busy in the kitchen.
To his surprise he was communicating
with the kitchen crew using sign language.
Jonathan knew the new restaurant's name
and asked if that would be Billy himself.
"Yes," Sally said, "that's my Billy of Billy's Balloons.
It is a cute name for our place we think.
This is our daughter Fairhope.
She will show you to your table."

As for Cameron and Gus, well, they were
at a corner table eating crab cakes,
taking in the whole scene with amazement.
Summer Reyes would be coming next week,
and they would be back.

3

Celebrations

American Acropolis

Atop the steep green hill
massive sides of ancient board
gleam in the bright sun.
She is huge, she captures
the landscape, holds the eye.
Her shadows define
shapes pleasing enough
to rival the fairest mean.
The great barn seems a temple
for the goddesses Gaea and Demeter,
the place where nature's full
fecundity finds a grateful host.

Sarah's Farewell

Now comes new winter's day
the shortest of the year
Not much time to say
goodbye to those held dear

The path to Sarah's house
is filled now with snow
A good one to bitch and grouse
she said it's time for me to go

And so she just stopped eating
and convened a celebration
She stood at the door a-greeting
the whole damn congregation

All her friends came that day
Their feelings were complex
Some felt nothing but dismay
Some danced the ice-cold deck

Calmly and peacefully one day
with people who loved her dearly
she silently slipped away her way
Sarah knew her mind so clearly

It is easy to miss someone
who loved my cooking so
On this day of little sun
I feel an afterglow

We thought she was full gone
but I found a message in her desk
"Miss me but do not mourn
I lived well and better than the rest"

Spring Suspended

Hovering, waiting,
she has held back

Spring suspended

No viridescent
displays cover
the still gray woods

The snow has gone
but crocuses
are all there is
to signal change

Perhaps she cannot
bear the thought of
arriving to know
that Ned has gone

Celebration

Of some it has been said,
"We'll not see his likes again."
With Ned we knew that
long before the end.

Raconteur! Provocateur!
He entranced, amused, cajoled,
entertained by tales both new and old.
The man could tease and charm,
hardly anyone he could not disarm.

An entrepreneur as well!
Selling Jeeps in Asia,
farming chickens in Nigeria,
trying with wind machines
long before wind's day had come.

He was the real deal:
curious, engaged, present.
"I've been thinking," Ned said
one day, nearly ninety-four,
"about a new approach
to climate change."

He loved his family, his town,
loved life, loved women,
loved all of us,
really cared about us,
asked often after us.

A dear, witty, and very wise man
who gained age with grace
and grace with age.
He had the world's best smile.
No pomp or pretention
but nothing average either.
None of him average.
Not the smallest smidgen.

Happy Ending. Not!

The beach was fabulous.
It could have been salubrious
for all us youngcoupolous.
But we drank superfluous.
Grip on reality got tenuous,
self-control became laborious,
hand driving car was tremulous,
skidding was furious,
so that was the end of us,
far beyond neosporious.
Remorseful now, all of us—
heaven not so bounteous,
food not really scrumptious,
the lectures very ponderous.
God makes fun of us.
He makes us abstemious!
We are just incredulous.
An ending ignominious.

Springtime

Winter has had a very long run.
Welcoming this bright spring sun,
I'll go looking for early green.
First, I'll check for rhubarb's sheen,
then for tiny grass where it's clear,
the smell of detritus in the air,
the early buds of daffodils
poking here and there on our hills.

I've done this now for many years.
It lubricates my rusty gears.
I wonder what manner of mind
could live in April and yet find
her to be the month most cruel.
Is it but the poet saying April Fool?
It seems it's something far more deep:
depression prefers the winter's sleep.

Friendship

She was an old dog,
hard of seeing, hearing,
and an awful winter:
snow rain melt freeze,
snow rain melt freeze—
everything slick with ice.
The old man let her out
to do her business.
He saw her standing
at the edge of the yard,
the big hill dropping
fast down to the woods,
a steep sledding slope
for the grandkids.

A glance later she was gone.
One step too far, with
ancient limbs and no traction,
she had slid away.

He dressed hurriedly
and spotted her trapped
in a jumble of bramble
down at the bottom,
occasionally struggling
but with no effect.
The old man's back was afflicted,
painful and giving out.
Still he headed down,
stumbling to the bottom.

The dog seemed glad
to have him by her side.
He was glad to be there too.
He lifted her big Lab body
and started up the hill.
When the pain was too great,
he paused, let it subside,
remembered she had been
an acrobat at Frisbee, had
loved to play with the ducks.

He thought: two elder residents
of town in trouble and now
struggling together to get
up a hill covered with ice.
What could be better?

He lifted her one last time
as they approached the stone steps
to the house, and it was too much.
His feet slipped out from under him,
the dog let loose as he reached for the ice.
His head landed inches from the steps.
He rolled over, looked up, and grinned
as she stood licking his face.

Delmarva

a truly great spot that
America most forgot
you have won our hearts again
thank you for the oysters
and the crabs and the clams and the ponies
thank you a lot
lord how the kids loved the ponies
the foal by the road has our hearts

after being away a long time
we are again the two of us
walking on Assateague
a beach so long it's the
whole of Maryland's shore
and so pristine its
sands sparkle and squeak
laughing gulls laughing with us
breakers breaking fast
into the sand's steep slope
a beautiful blue and pale green
and a boy asleep in warm dunes

behind the beach are the marshes
the marshes are owned by the birds
birds are the best of what's left
across the marsh on the island
is quaint Chincoteague town
oh god there are pieces still here
of what the watermen had once

the small lovely houses
and the big boats and the little boats
and the nets and the pots
big men in wet trousers
and the smell of old fish
ripe on the docks

but big houses are moving in now
Marriott and lots more are
commandeering the island's shore
the great American machine
is colonizing little Chincoteague
an eager participant we surmise
in her own oncoming demise

All the Color

Don't think that the colors you see
streaking across the high ceiling
spread wide by a glass award
now sitting in the window sill
are all the colors.

There are other colors and other awards.

There's an award of pure white
for the endless gifts you bestowed
on family, friends, even strangers.
What is love if not
caring unreservedly
and giving regardless?

There's a flat black award
for sitting quietly and absorbing
all that is going on in the world
and then standing up straight
and acting with strong purpose.
The actual size of the purpose
does not matter all that much.
It is the transcendence that does.

Then the rust-colored award
for gracefully aging-in-place
without too much complaint.

And the phthalo-green award
for repeated acts of eco-tage,
large and small, legal and illegal.

We do not see, much less live,
the true spectrum of all the colors
until life explodes like a collapsing star
and the higher elements with
all their density are born.

A Dog's Life

What do the dogs most enjoy,
other than eating of course?
What do they demand with
wet noses and come-on nudges?

Bright in the mornings,
they chase the ball with
abandon and aplomb.
Proudly, they catch it in the air
and find it lost in the grasses.

It is not the exercise,
nor the praise, but
the sheer joy of accomplishment—
doing what they do well
when they are up for magic.

Later in the day as
boredom creeps in on napping,
they want to explore
the world more slowly.

A walk down the road
and into the woods,
to see where the grouse hide,
to find some blackberries,
to smell every possible thing,
tails going like metronomes.

Pride in their competence,
joy from their curiosity,
oh, these are just simple animals,
lacking the higher powers.

Fast Breeder

The student takes me head on
as I'm talking my Luddite talk.
"Really," he says, "what new tech
has ever been beaten?!"

I reel as I feel time unfold,
travelling back fifty years
to the day the White House said,
"Our best hope lies with the
Fast Breeder Reactor."

"The what?" the students say.
Half-century earlier
we greens said, "No way!"

The breeder, you see, produces
more fuel than it uses.
That sounds like a premium,
but that fuel is plutonium.
It's bomb material, to be shipped
all across an energy-guzzling land,
hundreds of breeders coming by 2000.
To friends and foes alike
it's named the "plutonium economy."

It took ten hard years to beat the beast.
If you've never heard of it, that's why.

4

The Proper Order of the World

Holding It All Together

I can't imagine
the world working
when I'm gone
or if I just quit.

The guidance I give
shouting at the TV,
cursing in the yard,
advising friends what to think,
giving assignments to reporters,
holds the world together,
such as it is.

Coping is what it's all about.
Pissing in the wind,
whistling past the graveyard,
these are life skills
learned in lesser times
and now invoked.

As the proper order of the world
seems rather threatened,
and the supplies of comity,
discretion, and common decency run short,
still, we will confound the world
with civility and thoughtful observation
while going berserk at home
where oaths echo
from wall to wall.

New Morning

Now with the shove of pill bottles
into the drawer for another stay,
I will appear to all who care
an average guy greeting another day.

Do all of us have our
drug store displays?
Who knows what's
truly average?

Whatever!
Here today I'm ready
for anything it brings,
pills in the drawer and the cabinet,
ready to dethrone the king.

Feet unsteady, I stumble around.
Poet Thomas says I must rage.
No one notices how I'm
entering my anecdotage.

Is the long travail nearly over,
the seamless hours of striving?
I doubt it, but an easy thought
for a new day in the morning.

airborne

first bounce dogs
they are jumping
levitating defying
all constraints
they own the ball

a great catch
they know it
and hustle back
with a little swagger

scientists test to see
if dogs do have
human emotions
good lord
they would do better
to test humans

Not Far From the Tree

He saw it coming,
saw the wreckage coming,
wreckage driven ever on
and on by the warming,
the rising, and the changing.
Saw it early, decades ago,
and he cried out,
thinking they would listen.
He saw then that it was
the heart that would decide.
He cried to a big world
from a small pulpit.

Young then and hopeful,
hopeful that words would matter,
words could reach the heart.
And so he wrote, invoking
the whole life community
that evolved here with us—
life we did not create and
over which we are not lord.

Years later, as an old man,
he challenged his few readers
to imagine Earth without us.
When asked why he would
even think such a thing, he said,
consider the wreckage
gathering at your feet.
Does it not break your heart?

Now pause, he said, be still,
and contemplate such a world:
living canopies so vast
a small squirrel can move in trees
from the Delaware to the Mississippi,
oceans so fish-filled there appear
to be paths across the water,
flocks of passenger pigeons that
cast large shadows on the landscape,
great herds of ungulates
grazing across cool savannahs,
an Earth thriving with diversity.

But without us.
It's a test, he said, of our
environmental imagination.
If we can imagine such a world
with feelings of awe and reverence,
taking joy in its existence
even though we are no part of it,
nature for nature's sake,
then we are ready
to answer a question.

What is a species worth?
Perhaps just a small part
of nature's tapestry?
It depends on what is
vital and alive to you,
what your imagination sees.

Place yourself, the old man urged,
not as superior to nature
but as evolution's child,
close kin to wild things,
part of nature's flourishing,
threads in the tapestry.
Then you will know the answer.
The heart will decide.

The Evening News

These days the evening news fills
my brain and other vacant spaces
with disgust and deep loathing.
Sometimes there is real fury.
All the decades of good work:
how did it come to this?

The evening news, of course, begins
at 8 a.m. with Amy Goodman. Already
she has worked up a simmering scorn.

Then it picks up again at noon, when
Andrea Mitchell is on and has
steeled herself with incredulity.
She is followed closely by
the irreverently bemused Jake Tapper.
Jake is great at spotting hypocrites,
of which he finds no shortage.

Then, there are the weather and other
catastrophes brought to us on the
actual evening news by Lester Holt.
He tries desperately to show us
the world is not really falling apart,
even though it certainly seems that way.

All this negativity
rattles my positivity,
sapping my old age strength.

Perhaps I should just relax
and turn on the late news.
It may be time for Rachel.

Smoky

She sat there on the toasted bagel
wild and smoky and sassy as you like,
and looked me in the eye and said,
Could you give me some good EVOO
rather than that cream cheese?
And I said sure, whatever you want.
You must not be from the city?
No, she said, but nearby.
And then she asked, do you have
some fine chopped red onion?
Sure, I said, that's a good choice.
And while I was getting the onion,
she said, since you are up,
please get some capers too.
And rinse them if you don't mind.
I don't mind at all, not a bit.
You must be going out today, I said.
Yes, she replied. My friend is giving a party
and I want to look nice—my best.
I hope you have a good time, I said.
Yes, she said, with a sly little smile.
We have been friends a long time
and I try not to ever let him down.
Would you like pepper? I asked.
Honey, she said, pepper I do not need.

Forgiveness

I have some vivid memories
I wish were not there

We heard it all the time
in the South in the '50s
That's mighty white of you!
racist words spoken then
as just a casual thank you

I went recently to the
Blacksonian on the Mall
and I left there uplifted
but with moist eyes and cheeks
When I got home I listened
to King speak in Memphis
"I've been to the mountaintop"

Gnawing away inside me are
the shootings at Mother Emanuel
the many times Black lives haven't mattered
the mass incarceration
the famine of equal opportunity
the ongoing everyday prejudice

I want to go in supplication
to the Calhoun Street sidewalk
to the Edmund Pettus bridge
to Montgomery's memorial
to four thousand lynchings
and ask there for a forgiveness
that in acts of amazing grace has
already been given so many times

Crepuscular Thoughts

I was thinking of a happy ending,
but took a break and went to watch
the giant project of "beach renourishing,"
a project I would have loved to scotch.

Slurried ashore in three giant pipes,
the sand intended to shore up the beach.
That of course was all just tripe:
the new sand soon in sea level's reach.

Where the waves now lap at condo doors,
the poem somehow slipped from my hand
and disappeared there along the shore
swept away under tons of dirt brown sand.

Fishing with the Family

There once was a boat that the salesman said
was solely owned by the preacher.
"He used it on Sundays after church
to take out his wife, the teacher."
Out on charming Chincoteague Bay

I remember it all with a sense of dread.
Every last word that salesman said
went straight into my gullible head.
Embarrassment can still turn me red.
Out on charming Chincoteague Bay

Never buy a new boat or an old motor,
that's the sage advice from my father.
I could have listened a great deal better
and thus greatly reduced my bother.
Out on charming Chincoteague Bay

The motor died early one Sunday
fishing with my family that day
far into Chincoteague Bay.
The good news is, I'm pained to say,
the Coast Guard was not too far away.
Out on charming Chincoteague Bay

A Balanced Life

The soul is more important than the back

A child rushes towards you
Little arms outstretched
Pick up the child

The sun graces the morning beach
It goes for miles
Walk the beach

The dogs insist on Frisbee
The motion's like a hula hoop
Throw it hard

The exercises prescribed
Awake real pain
Do them…sometimes

Your partner's car arrives
With bags of groceries
Head for the bathroom

The Promise

the snow's just gone, the moment feels unreal
the earth is pat down gray and brown
a porcupine moves slowly through our field
headed somewhere between lost and found

nothing too dramatic going on
so much of life seeming gone
spring held in check again
spates of warming asking when
left bears and sap turning round
wondering do I now head up or down

I saw a sugar house last night
late but all cranked up despite
bright and busy with the boiling
beer and banter slake the toiling
these times worth remembering

climate change is messing with the season
messing too with plain reason
the climate models are predicting
that maples will be disappearing
what's left, what's green we must hold tight
no, not going gently without a fight

www.ingramcontent.com/pod-product-compliance
Lightning Source LLC
Chambersburg PA
CBHW030532080526
44586CB00011B/408